Presents
money can't buy

Sheridan Simove

summersdale

PRESENTS MONEY CAN'T BUY

Text and illustrations by Sheridan Simove

Condition of Sale

Summersdale Publishers Ltd
46 West Street
Chichester
West Sussex
PO19 1RP
UK

www.summersdale.com

Printed and bound by Tien Wah Press, Singapore

ISBN: 1-84024-496-8
ISBN: 978-1-84024-496-0

BREAKING NEWS! IT REALLY *IS* THE THOUGHT THAT COUNTS…

If you want to show someone how much they mean to you, then use the most powerful organ in your body: your brain. Giving a meaningful present isn't just about splashing your cash on flowers, chocolates or a gift token – these are far too easy and clichéd! This book gives you practical ideas for a wide range of gifts that will really make someone's day. So pick one now and make them feel really special…

BOTTLED SUNSHINE

Take a small jar and go outside on a sunny day. Put the lid on the jar and then label it 'Bottled Sunshine'. When someone you care about needs cheering up, give them the bottle wrapped up in some tissue paper. Tell them that they are like bottled sunshine to you.

COMPLETE MUG

Make someone a coffee and serve it in a mug you've designed. Many photographic shops will now print mugs for you, so just tell them what you need and they'll create a unique piece of crockery sure to be treasured. Alternatively, you can buy 'paint your own mug' sets.

Ideas for what you can print on the mug:

Their name:	e.g. JUDY'S MUG
A picture:	An image that means something to the recipient or you both
Preference:	e.g. Dave likes his tea white with two sugars
A slogan:	e.g. You're just like my coffee: hot, strong & black!

NET RESULT

Create a web page with a special message displayed on it and then send your recipient a link to it. There are dozens of sites on the Internet that let you build a small website for free. Just type 'FREE WEBSITE' or 'FREE WEB PAGE' into any search engine to get started. Most of them have templates that make it very simple to build your own site. The website will be accessible from anywhere in the world and only someone who is told the address you created for it will know where to find it.

UNLOCK A GREAT GIFT IDEA

Create a keepsake that someone can carry around on a keyring or a neck chain. Visit a locksmith, choose a key you like and then ask for the key to be engraved with a word or phrase of your choosing.

ALCOHOLIDAY

Create a specially designed 'Hangover Kit' for someone you know is soon to enjoy an intoxicating night out, whether it be a special celebration or just a fun weekend out on the tiles. Buy a gift box and place the following objects inside:

* A bottle of water (create your own label)
* Some headache tablets
* A token for a free full English breakfast from your local greasy spoon café
* A note from you

MEAL-LY INDULGENT

Instead of just cooking a meal for someone, make sure it's a night they'll never forget by turning your dining room into your own restaurant. Put a sign up on the wall with the name of your restaurant on it and write or print a menu. Dim the lights, light some candles and serve the meal… You can even dress up as a member of waiting staff if you like! (Just don't give them a bill, obviously.)

POST MODERN

If you really want to wow someone when you send them a letter or greeting card, put a stamp on the envelope that you've designed yourself. The Royal Mail offers a service whereby you can get your own stamps made – you give them the image and then they send you your stamp. Log on to www.royalmail.co.uk and find 'SMILERS®'.

INK-REDIBLE

A unique little gift is to present someone with their very own temporary tattoo. Just type 'TATTOO PRINTING PAPER' into a search engine to find suppliers. You can then create a temporary tattoo of any image or slogan you desire by simply using an inkjet computer printer to print onto the special paper. The person you give it to can put it on with water and wash it off with soap.

GROW FOR IT

Here's how to make somebody a highly unusual present that's good enough to eat. Simply buy some salad cress seeds from any garden centre, place a sheet of wet kitchen paper or moistened cotton wool on a plate and sprinkle the seeds in the shape of the person's initial on the wet surface. Then, when the seeds have sprouted, you'll have a wonderful cress initial. Healthy and personalised!

GET THEM PANT-ING

Buying gorgeous underwear for someone is always a great gift. But you can make the present all the more memorable with an extra twist – personalise your purchase with their name. Ask a shop specialising in embroidery to stitch on the name of the person you're giving the underwear to. Then give the person in question their very own one-of-a-kind undies!

POP IDOLISE

It's great to receive an anthology of music that's been hand-picked just for you. But you can take the idea of making a compilation tape/CD even further: before each song, record yourself saying why it means something to you or why you've chosen it for the recipient. Then design a unique cover insert for your personal album.

Great to look at,
And Delicious too,
In fact this sandwich
is just like you!

USE YOUR LOAF

Here's how to make a deliciously different packed lunch gift: make a sandwich for someone with all their favourite fillings. Then use a shaped cookie cutter (available from most kitchen utensil shops) and cut out your special sandwich in a heart shape. Wrap it in foil and stick a note on top.

JEANIUS

Make someone a fashion garment they'll never forget. First find out what size jeans they wear and buy a pair in their size from a charity shop or from an Internet auction; then make the gift a completely personal work of art by adding flashes of unusual material and colourful buttons, both available from craft shops or textile stores. If you can't sew, simply take the jeans and the extra accessories to a local dry cleaning firm that specialises in alterations and they'll be happy to bring your vision to life.

DREAM ON

If you're away from someone you care about for a long time, then make sure they can still kiss you goodnight by creating your very own forget-me-not pillow – a pillowcase with your face on it! Choose your best photo and take a pillowcase to a printer's to get the image transferred onto the material. Alternatively, buy some iron-on printer paper so you can apply the image yourself.

A FRYDAY TO TREASURE

Make someone their very own personalised packet of crisps. Simply slice a large potato thinly and then cut the slices into shapes with some scissors. Some suggestions for shapes are circles, stars or even hearts. Then deep fry the shaped slices in hot oil, drain and place in a small plastic sandwich bag covered with a label you've made.

LOVE IS BLINDS

Create a picture or message on a large piece of paper, then cut the paper into strips and stick them onto some closed blinds with Blu Tack, attaching one strip per slat. Then open the blinds so the image cannot be seen. When someone closes the blinds, all the slats will line up and your creation will miraculously appear!

PIZZA THE ACTION

Send a gift they'll never forget: call a pizza delivery firm and find out if they'll customise a pizza. Ask them to spell a name on the pizza using olives, anchovies or asparagus (or whatever the recipient's favourite ingredients are) and then get the culinary token delivered to the person you're surprising.

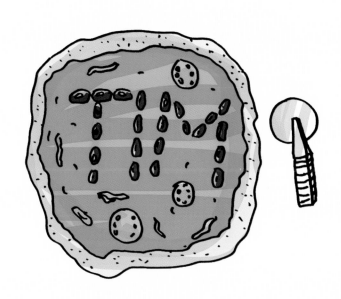

BALLOONATIC

Create a floating trail of balloons indoors, each with a special note inside. Before filling each of the balloons, write a note and place it inside. Then set up the first balloon and position near it a small box (like one from a jewellery store that was used to hold a ring) containing a single pin. Put a sign up explaining that to read the notes from you, the balloons must be popped one by one.

GO NUTS

Buy a small piece of jewellery – a ring or a pair of earrings, for example – and then make the presentation all the more special by trying out this idea. Carefully crack open a walnut, remove the edible nut, insert the piece of jewellery and add a tiny dab of craft glue (the type used by children) to each half of the nut so that the two pieces of shell are joined back together, but can be easily prised open when the gift is presented. Tie the sealed nut with a ribbon and hand it to your lucky special friend.

CAROMA

Make a pair of personalised car air fresheners that will remind someone of you every time they get a whiff of the sweet scent. Buy two hanging air fresheners from a petrol station and cut them out into a person's initials. Then wrap them up in some wrapping paper with a suitable note for a fun and fragrant gift.

TOKEN GESTURE

Give a tangible token of your love. Take a large foreign coin or a casino chip and create your own label to stick in the middle. The label should include these words:

ONE LOVE TOKEN
VALUE: PRICELESS

Hand it to someone with a note that proclaims 'This is a token of my love'.

EVERYONE'S A WINNER

Award someone a trophy just for being them. Look in the Yellow Pages for your nearest trophy shop. Most shops of this kind sell generic trophies – get one engraved with a suitably personal message that celebrates something unique about the person you're giving it to.

REFLECTED GLORY

Buy an A4 sheet of clear plastic that you can print on using an inkjet printer. You can purchase these sheets from most stationers – they're designed for overhead presentations. Simply print a message on one sheet, cut it to size and stick it to a mirror with some tiny pieces of clear sticky tape. Because the plastic is clear it'll look like the words are printed on the mirror.

WASH UPON A SPA

Give the gift of a wonderful pampering soak. Buy a bottle of bath oil from any supermarket or chemist and take a small washcloth to a shop that offers embroidery and arrange to have a message or a name sewn on it (or sew it yourself if you can!). Finally, ask your local florist if they can supply you with fresh flower petals or buy some flowers and strip them for their petals. Place these petals in a small, attractive net bag, or even a plain plastic sandwich bag will do. Put everything in a small basket (available from a florist or gift shop) and tie a silk bow around the whole ensemble. Voilà! A beautiful spa kit for your special someone – give it right away while the petals are fresh.

FOWL PLAY

Customise a toy that will make someone smile every time they take a bath. Buy a yellow plastic duck from a children's or home store and use a permanent marker to decorate or write a message on the duck, thus creating a one-of-a-kind bath-time ornament.

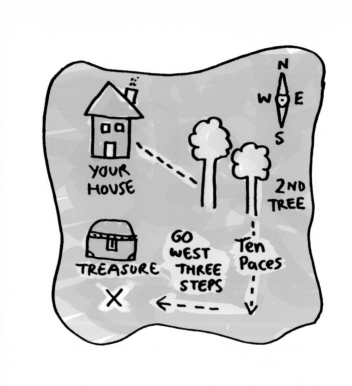

TREASURE MY-LAND

Send someone on a simple treasure hunt, letting them discover trinkets and messages you've hidden in their home, workplace or local area. Draw a map of their house, office or nearby landmarks to lead them to the treasures one by one. Kick-start the treasure hunt by e-mailing someone a cryptic clue or a simple instruction like, 'Look in your glove compartment'.

MAKE YOUR MARK

Give someone their very own personalised bookmark. Simply cut out a piece of card in a bookmark shape and cover it with cut-up photos or even a cartoon strip from a newspaper that means something to both of you. For a really professional finish, you could even get it laminated at a print shop.

THE DAILY MEL
EXCLUSIVE!
MELANIE HAS BIRTHDAY
FULL STORY PAGES 1-10

PAPER VIEW

For a special occasion like an anniversary or birthday, make someone their very own newspaper front page. Simply cut out individual letters from existing newspaper headlines and paste them together to create your own relevant headline. Then add a photo of your recipient and a short news story about them to finish the effect. You may want to stick the finished spread on an existing paper and have it delivered, or even get it framed so that the person receiving it can hang it in their home.

HOLLYWOOD
YOU BELIEVE IT

Here's how to give someone a 'night at the movies' experience in their own home. Place the following in a shoebox: a feature film on DVD that you know the person will enjoy watching; a bag of popcorn; two cans of fizzy drink; and some assorted packets of sweets. For the finishing touch, ask your local fast-food outlet if they'll give you two large, unused paper cups and cover the cups with homemade labels indicating popcorn.

CHOCS AWAY

Most people adore chocolate, so here's how to make a chocolate treat that's sure to delight. Melt two big bars of chocolate in a heatproof bowl placed over a saucepan of boiling water. Then pour the melted chocolate into letter or shape moulds (available from kitchenware stores) and allow to cool. Next, put the moulds in the fridge so that the chocolate sets solid. Later remove the moulds and place them briefly in a bowl of shallow warm water – your chocolate creations will then easily slide out onto a plate, leaving you to make your own unique chocolatey words and pictures.

COCOA NUTS

Cut out a symbol, such as a heart or an initial, from a beer mat or any stiff card of roughly the same size. Then make a hot chocolate or milky coffee. Cover the drink with thick whipped cream, carefully pat it down with the back of a teaspoon to create an even surface and dust the top with cocoa powder, holding the template over the cup so that the shape appears on the cream.

THE REAL DEAL

Make someone a totally original pack of
playing cards. Buy a cheap deck of cards,
remove the king or queen of diamonds,
then cut out the person's face from a
photo and stick it onto the playing card
over the existing illustrated face. Write a
message with the cards, e.g., 'You're a
diamond geezer'.

EMOTIONAL BAGGAGE

Create a very special luggage tag for someone when they're about to travel away from home. Cut out a rectangle from a cereal box. Stick a photo or funny picture onto one side of the card and on the other write the name and contact details of the person you're giving it to. Take the card to a printing shop and ask for it to be laminated so that it'll be smartly protected whilst in transit. Punch a hole in the corner of the tag and thread a piece of strong string or ribbon through the hole. Give your travelling recipient the tag and wish them '*bon voyage*'!

VOUCH FOR THEM

Make a voucher that's specially tailored to the person you're giving it to. Picking something you know to be important or amusing to them, design a coupon with an explanation of what it's valid for. Tell them you'll honour the voucher and that they can cash it in any time they wish.

Voucher ideas...

* Valid for one breakfast in bed
* Valid for one bout of washing up
* Valid for one evening's entertainment of your choice

EGG-SHELL-ENT IDEA

Surprise your loved one by making them a personalised boiled egg. Simply boil an egg (six minutes should do it, or four if you want it runny), then dry the egg and use a non-toxic felt tip or a drywipe marker pen (used on white boards) to carefully draw a face or write a message onto the shell. Serve with toast soldiers and a personal message:

'Maddie, you *crack* me up!'

'You get me all *egg-cited*, Peter'

'I can't get *an-oeuf* of you, María'

MAJOR EGGBERT AND HIS TOAST SOLDIERS

GARY'S
Horoscope
Today, you will meet a gorgeous blonde called Miranda Make sure you buy her some new shoes...
—x—

STARS IN YOUR EYES

Become an amateur astrologer by creating a horoscope for someone you care about. Buy some dark writing paper from a gift shop and at the same time purchase a pen that writes in silver or gold ink. Use the pen to write out someone's personal horoscope for a particular day: put their name at the top and then invent a prediction of what will happen to them for the next twenty-four hours. Pop your horoscope in a fancy envelope and deliver it to your intended recipient.

IN THE FRAME

Create a lasting memory of the first time you met someone, or perhaps a first date, by framing a receipt or a concert ticket from that special day. Beneath the receipt or ticket, write a strapline that neatly commemorates the occasion, e.g., 'Our First Date at the Movies – You'll Always be my Leading Man / Lady'. If you don't have the original receipt or ticket, then just get a menu, logo or picture of the place you went to and frame that instead.

THE FOOD OF LOVE

Here's how to prepare a simple but unique snack surprise: toast one piece of bread, warm up a tin of alphabet spaghetti and spell out a message with the spaghetti on the toast. Serve.

HOLIDAY HOME

Create a realistic indoor beach for someone to relax on by clearing a room of furniture and placing a thick plastic sheet down on the floor. Then simply set up a sun lounger or deckchair on the sheet and lay a large beach towel down. Add to the scene any other seaside items you like: some clean pebbles, shells, a rubber ring, a bucket and spade – and, if you think your surprised recipient will appreciate it, some fine sand bought from a builders' yard or garden centre and a small inflatable paddling pool filled with water. Put an extra heater in the room and turn it up so that the temperature rises to tropical heights. Finally, place a sign on the door that reads: 'Life's a beach – and this one's just for you!'

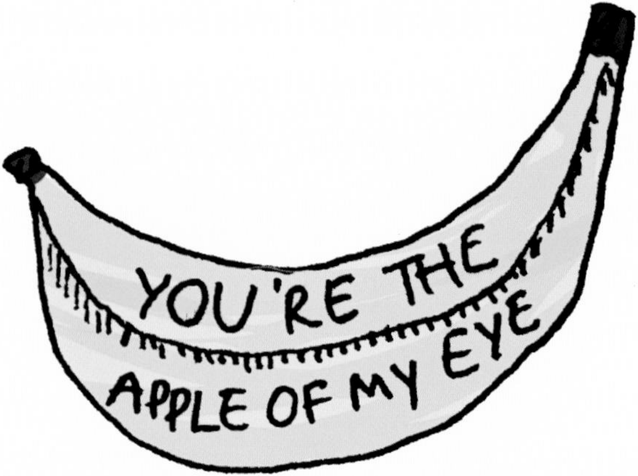
YOU'RE THE
APPLE OF MY EYE

FRUITFUL EXERCISE

Take a banana and a paperclip. Use the paperclip to lightly score a message on the skin of the banana. The parts of the skin you've marked with the paperclip will turn brown, resulting in a unique and healthy gift: a limited edition piece of banana art that can be enjoyed and then eaten! So go on – go bananas!

WHIFF YOU WERE HERE

Make someone their very own one-of-a-kind perfume or aftershave. Take a clean cloth and place it in the bottom of a soup bowl, then empty one cup of fresh chopped flower blossoms on top. Ask your local florist for some lavender, lilac, honeysuckle or even orange blossoms if they're available.

Pour a large cup of water over the blossoms and leave overnight. Then squeeze the water from the cloth into a saucepan and gently simmer the water for roughly an hour until the scent has concentrated. Once cool, pour the scent into a small glass bottle that you can buy from a beauty shop or chemist. Make a label for the bottle and it is ready to be given as a gift.

The fresh, aromatic concoction will last for about a month.

SIGN OF THINGS TO COME

Make someone their very own 'Do Not Disturb' sign for when they're busy. Take a piece of card and cut a hole in it so it fits onto a door handle. Next, write something appropriate on the card, like, 'Genius At Work' or 'Superwoman Busy – Do Not Enter'.

ICE IDEA

Make someone their very own personalised ice cubes. Buy some of your loved one's favourite sweets and then place them one by one in an ice tray. Hard sweets like jelly beans work the best. Cover the tray with water and freeze. Once you've created the personalised sweet ice cubes, serve them in a drink for your thirsty buddy.

LIVE AND LET DICE

Give someone their very own unique dice and then use them to have some fun! Take two square stock cubes and then place some small stickers (available from most stationers) on each side of the foiled cubes. Write commands on the stickers that are personal to you and the recipient. Arrange a games evening and then roll away…

BOX CLEVER

Buy a simple wooden box (you can find good ones in charity shops), then glue a collage of your favourite photos onto the box. Varnish the whole box with clear lacquer (available from most DIY shops) and you'll have created a completely original 'memory box' that will last for ages.

www.summersdale.com